Malia and Malachi Learn
The Importance of
Brushing Their Teeth

By Ella M. Daniels

This book is dedicated to all children.

The kids were scheduled to go to the park after school on Wednesday. Malachi loves to feed the ducks over there. Mom packed some bread in a basket to bring along.

Water

Arriving at the park, we saw a man running with his dog by his side. It was a **medium-sized** dog called a **German Shepard**. He was definitely keeping up with his owner.

Next to the duck pond was a lady sitting on a bench.
Malachi and Malia immediately noticed that she was
eating some snacks. She had a candy bar in her
hand. There was some **F**rench fries next to her on
the bench and a slice of cake **as well**.

"Mom, I want some candy and chips," said Malachi. "Can we go to the 7-11 store?" "Me too," said Malia. "No," replied Mom. "You don't need any junk food before dinner." "When we go home, you can get a healthier snack like a piece of fruit or even a peanut butter sandwich." "Just looking at her eating that stuff makes me want to brush my teeth when I get home." "You guys should too."

While they were standing there feeding the ducks, mom looked at her phone to research the benefits of brushing your teeth. Here is something I want to share with you guys.

She lets them know that:

There are benefits to brushing you teeth every day.
When you brush your teeth, you will be reducing the
tartar and plague that builds up on your teeth.

It will prevent gum disease as well as periodontitis (bacterial infection). It will lessen your chances of getting cavities while whitening your teeth.

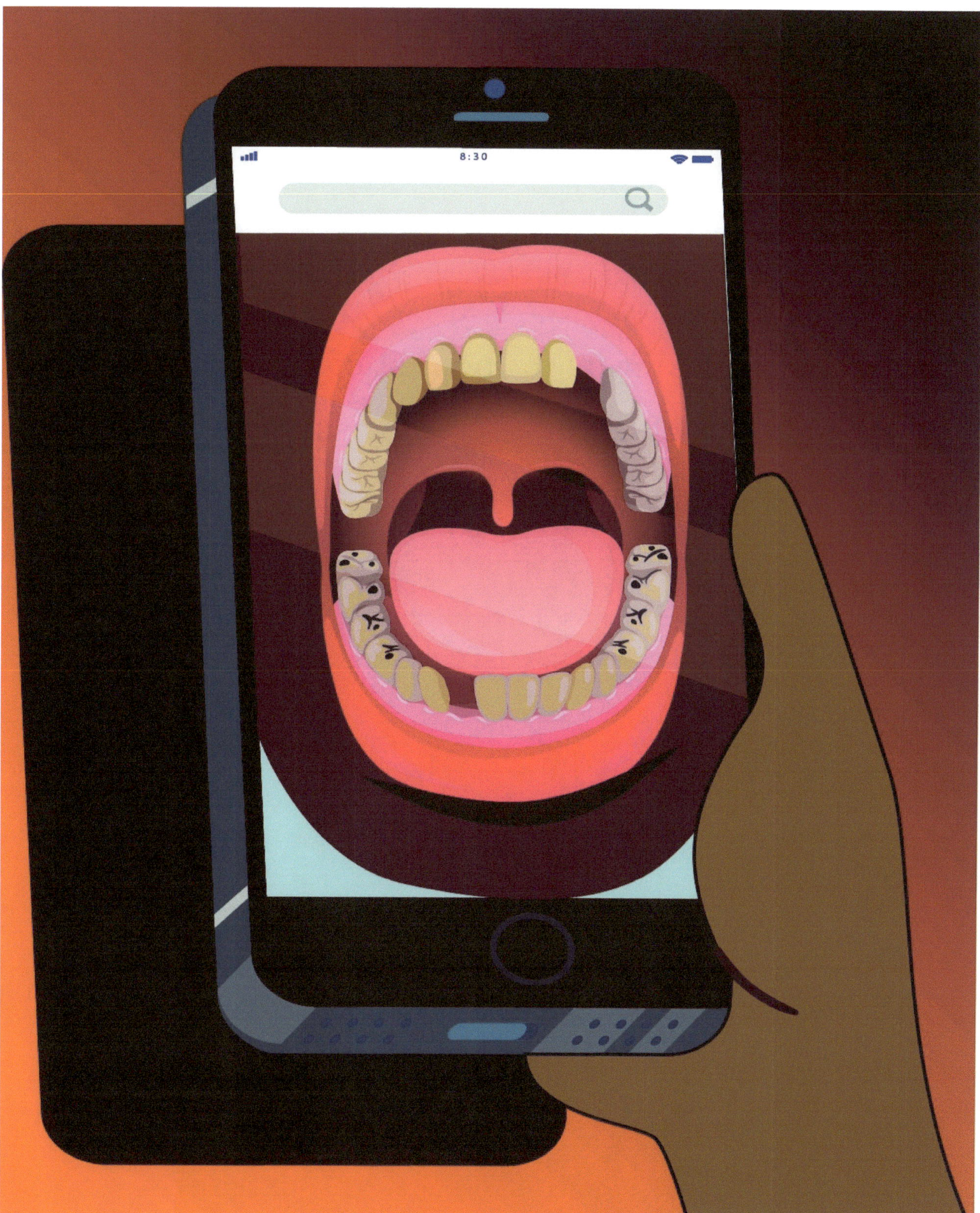
8:30

Your mouth is a gateway to the rest of your body.
Take care of it. A clean mouth will lessen your
chances of getting heart disease.

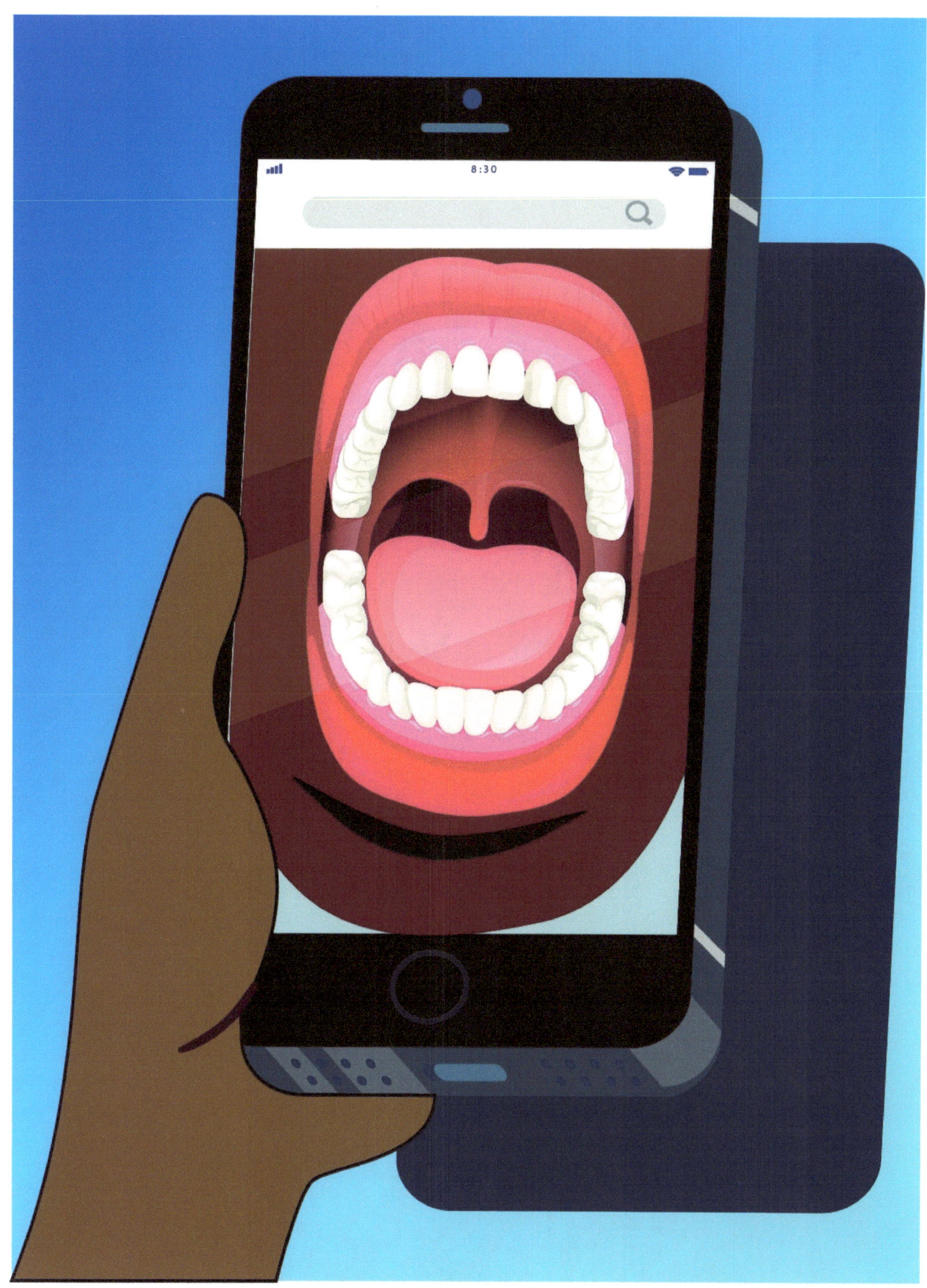

8:30

You should know that infections from poor oral health increases your chances of getting diabetes, and arthritis.

Diabetes- happens when your blood glucose level is too high.(type 2) Your pancreas can sometimes produce little or no insulin.(type1)

arthritis- inflammation in your joints.

Periodontitis disease comes from the bacteria that starts when plague is formed on and around your teeth.

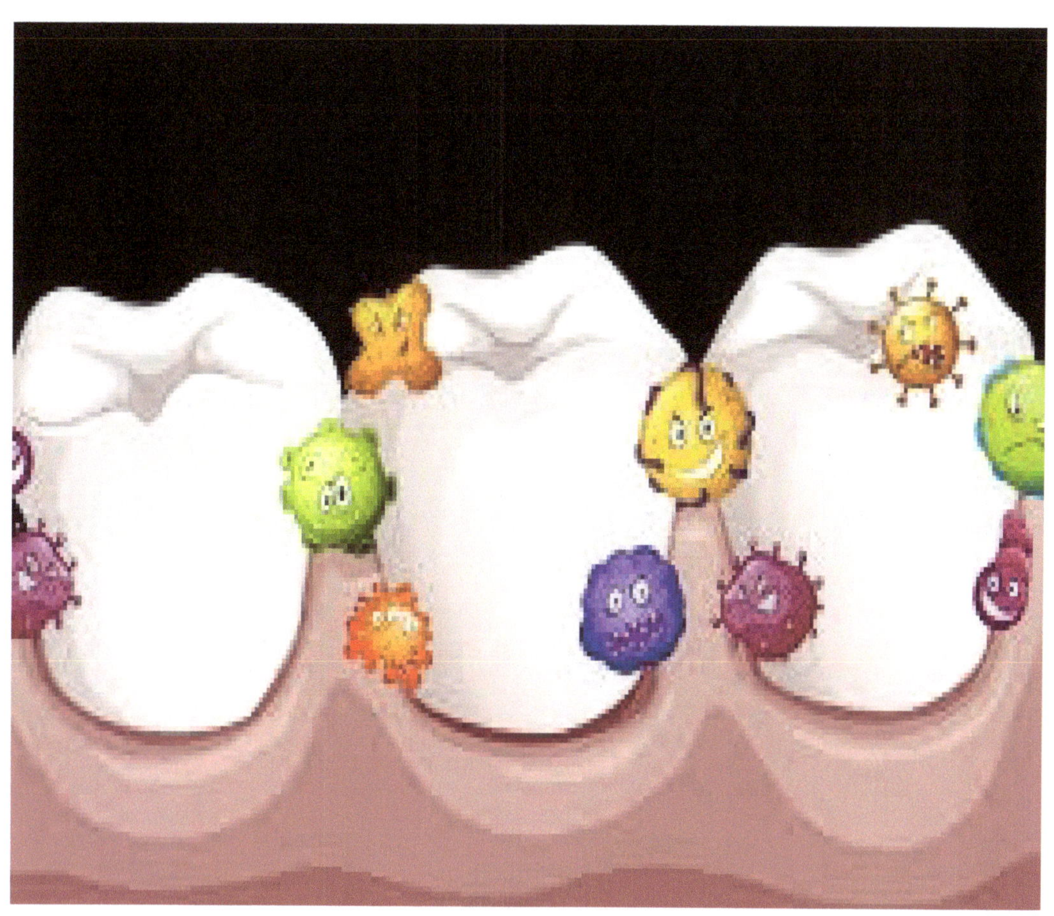

Periodontal disease

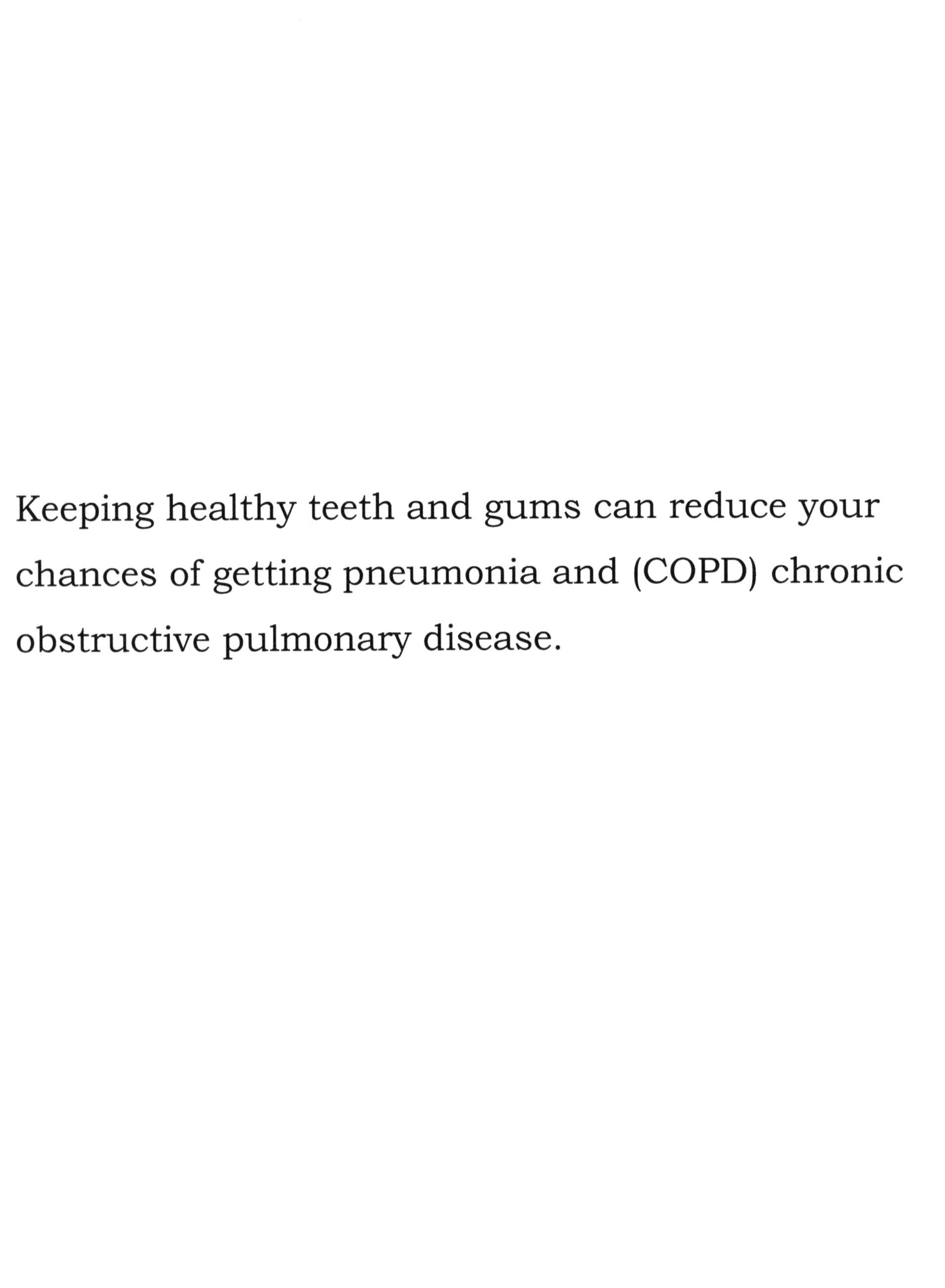

Keeping healthy teeth and gums can reduce your chances of getting pneumonia and (COPD) chronic obstructive pulmonary disease.

Pneumonia- infection of the air sacs in one or both of
a person's lungs

COPD- a group of lung diseases that make it hard to
breathe

There is research that connects gum disease with memory loss. Gingivitis bacteria can travel from your mouth to your brain. Protein is produced by the bacteria and it destroys nerve cells in the brain. There is medicine currently being developed that can block enzymes from the bacteria.

8:30

Mom said,"This is why I take the two of you to the dentist every year to get your dental checkups." "I want you guys to stay healthy and happy." "These are good habits that should last a lifetime."

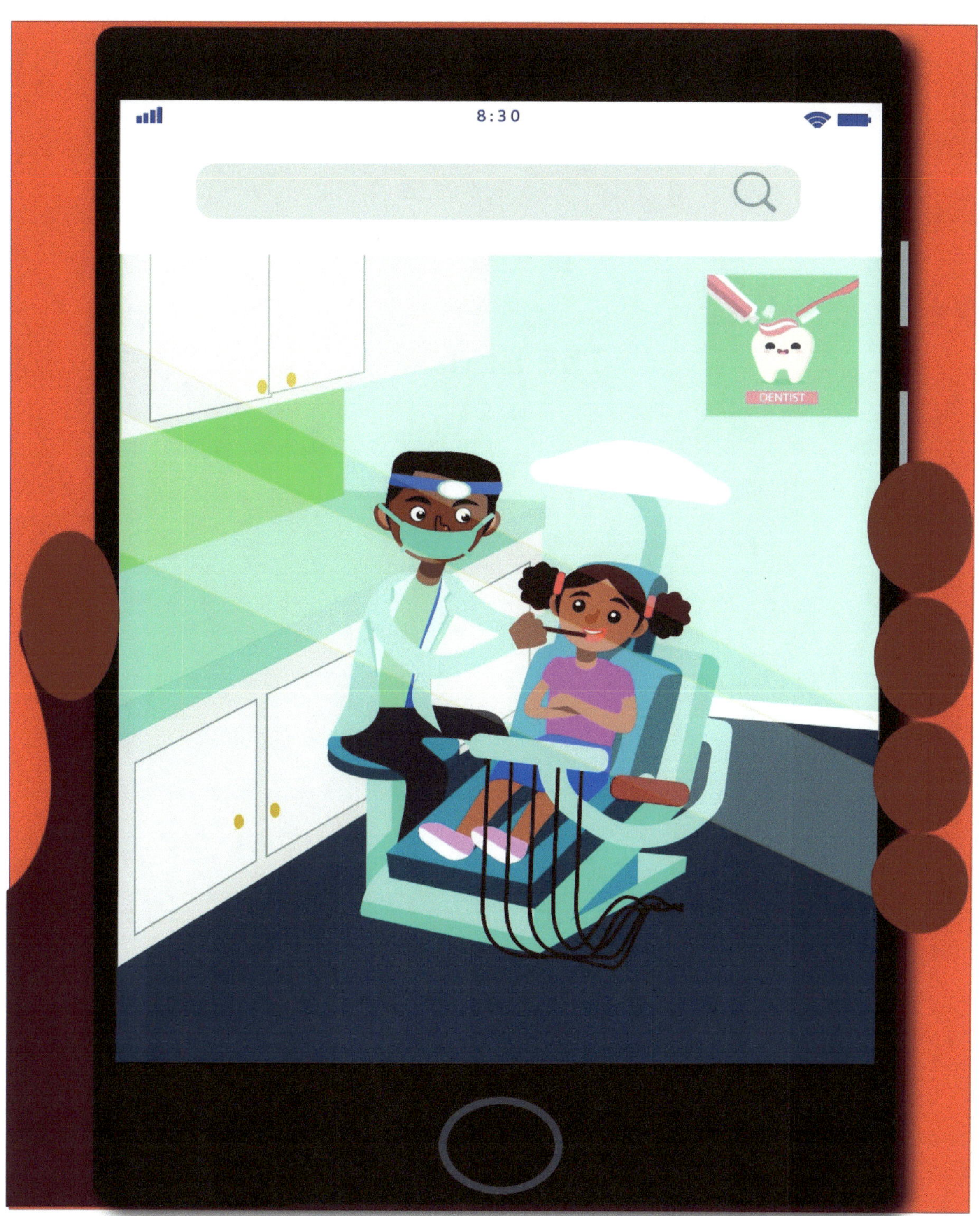
8:30
DENTIST

The End

Souces

1.
https://www.sciencedaily.com/releases/2011/01/110118143224.htm

2.
https://www.sciencedaily.com/releases/2016/08/160802104159.htm

3.
https://www.sciencedaily.com/releases/2019/06/190603102549.htm